D0184675

WEASELS IN THE ATTIC

HIROKO OYAMADA

WEASELS IN THE ATTIC

translated from the Japanese
by David Boyd

GRANTA

Granta Publications, 12 Addison Avenue, London W11 4QR

First published in Great Britain by Granta Books, 2022
Originally published in the United States in 2022 by New Directions Books,
New York

The stories in *Weasels in the Attic* were originally published in 2012, 2013, and 2014
by Shinchosha Publishing Co., Tokyo. This English edition is published
by arrangement with Shinchosha Publishing Co. in care
of Tuttle-Mori Agency, Inc., Tokyo.

The publisher gratefully acknowledges the support of JAPANFOUNDATION.

The translator would like to thank Nick Kapur and Rebekah Chacko.

A CIP catalogue record for this book is available from the British Library.

1 3 5 7 9 10 8 6 4 2

ISBN 978 1 78378 975 7
eISBN 978 1 78378 977 1

Design by Erik Rieselbach
Offset by Avon DataSet Ltd, Alcester, Warwickshire

Printed and bound by CPI Group (UK) Ltd, Croydon, CR0 4YY

www.granta.com

CONTENTS

DEATH IN THE FAMILY

I DIDN'T KNOW HOW TO RESPOND WHEN SAIKI CALLED TO tell me that Shuzo Urabe had died. I'd known Saiki since college, but Urabe was much more his friend than mine. I'd only met Urabe once, not that long ago, when Saiki and I went over to his place.

Saiki had just gotten back from the funeral, but it was pretty late.

"I just thought you should know . . ."

He hurried off the phone, and I opened a can of beer in Urabe's honor. As my mind started to clear, I realized something. It was last year, nearly six months ago, that we'd gone to Urabe's.

My wife had gone to bed ahead of me.

Urabe's family had a lot of money. I think he had two older brothers, and one of them had taken over the family company. Listening to Saiki, it sounded like Urabe had probably gone his whole life without ever having a real job. He was obsessed with tropical fish, so his family had set him up with his own fish shop. I guess they figured it would keep him busy. The business failed after a few years, but he still lived in the space above the shop.

Saiki was a fish lover, too. That was what they had in common.

"I used to have lots of fish, a long time ago. But then I went to Urabe's. He's a real collector. Guess it doesn't hurt that he's rich. Back when he had the shop, he had all the best tanks, the best fish. He told me I could have whatever I wanted, for free, but that kind of took the fun out of it."

"So you don't have any fish now?"

"Not anymore. Keeping them alive is way too much work."

One day, out of the blue, Saiki asked me to go to Urabe's with him. I had no idea why.

"He asked me to come out to his place. He said we had to celebrate a new addition to his family or something. I'd feel weird going alone, though."

When we met at the station, Saiki had a giant bottle of sake wrapped in fancy paper. I don't know why, but it hadn't occurred to me to bring anything. Noticing my concern, Saiki shook his head and lifted the bottle.

"We're covered. I told you, Urabe loves booze. This'll be more than enough. I mean, he could probably drink this whole bottle on his own, but we'll be fine, trust me."

I almost never drank, and I couldn't have cared less about tropical fish. From everything Saiki had told me, Urabe sounded really weird.

"Didn't he just have a baby? I don't know if we should be trying to get this guy wasted in front of his wife and kid."

"Whoa, hold up," Saiki laughed. "That's not what he meant by 'new addition.' At least I'm pretty sure it isn't. Urabe's not the marrying type. Hell, I'll tie the knot before he does. He probably just wants to show off some new fish or something. You'll see."

I wasn't sure if I was disappointed or relieved.

My wife and I had been together for three years, but we hadn't had any luck getting pregnant. She was always talking about fertility treatment, our "best options." These talks had basically become our nightly routine. Meanwhile, it was getting harder and harder for us to see other people our age with kids of their own.

"I always tell her it's her call. Then she comes back with all these pamphlets and websites. 'If the problem's on your side, here's what we can do, and here's what it'll cost us. If it's my womb, or my ovaries, here's what we can do, and here are our chances ...' It's the same thing every night. Then she asks me: 'On a scale of one to ten, how badly do you want kids?'"

"Man. What can you even say to that?"

When we got to Urabe's place, the old shop sign was still up over the door: WORLD OF WATER—RARE AND EXOTIC FISH. It was too dark to see anything through the window. There was some kind of plastic sheet hanging up on the other side of the glass. Saiki pushed the button on the intercom, then we went around the side and up the stairs to Urabe's apartment.

When we opened the door, Urabe was standing there. For some reason, I'd imagined that he was going to be some scrawny guy in glasses, but he was tall and had broad shoulders. He was actually pretty good-looking. I guess he was a little pale, but if somebody told me he used to wrestle, I'd believe it. His shirt had a wild pattern on it, the kind of thing a teenager would wear. I stepped inside and took off my shoes. Lining them up with the rest, I saw a pair that clearly belonged to a woman. I shot Saiki a look. He tilted his head like he had no clue who they belonged to either.

When we opened the door to what must've been his living room, the walls were lined with fish tanks, and standing in the middle of the room was a young woman, holding a baby in her arms, leaning a little to one side. She gave a sheepish nod hello.

"Okay, so when did this happen?"

Saiki's voice was higher than I'd ever heard. Urabe was already sitting on the couch, alone. He gave Saiki a baffled look. "What are you talking about? I told you on the phone."

"I thought you were talking about some new fish …" Saiki muttered under his breath.

Urabe glared at him, indignant.

"You really think I'm going to call you up every time I have some new fish to show you? Anyway, it's a girl. She was born last month."

Saiki looked embarrassed. I took a couple of steps toward the woman to get a better look at the baby, the way another woman might. "She's sleeping," Urabe's wife said, holding her child out. "Do you want to take her?" I nodded. The baby's face was small and red. Her shut eyes looked like knife slits. I could feel her warmth and dampness through the layers of cloth. I've always liked kids. I wished I could have one of my own. I couldn't give it a number, but I knew it was what I wanted.

Urabe's wife was wearing a soft, cottony blouse, her breasts hanging underneath. She and the baby really looked alike.

"She has your face," I said.

"You think so?" his wife asked. She had a few freckles on her cheeks, big eyes, and a small nose. Her daughter had the same nostrils.

Urabe's wife moved her tiny lips. "Her father says she doesn't."

"No, she does," I said. "She has your nose."

"My nose? … You really know how to hold her."

"My sisters have children, and I used to babysit for them all the time."

The way she giggled, she couldn't have been more than twenty. I held the baby for a while and then gave her back. She slept the whole time.

As soon as I handed the baby back, I noticed the tanks again. I didn't know anything about fish, but I could tell right away that this was no ordinary collection. The room had enough tanks to fill a whole shop. Maybe this had been his inventory back when the shop was open. The tanks had different shapes and sizes. The biggest one was rectangular, maybe five feet long. A few of the smaller ones were round. Some were filled with plants, but others were empty. Saiki and Urabe were standing in front of one of the tanks, talking about something.

"You think it's time?"

"Any minute now."

"Hmm. Look at them all."

"Yeah, they've got great chemistry."

I looked at the tank. There were two round, flat fish inside. They were silver with inky vertical stripes, about six inches long. Depending on how the light hit, their scales glowed green or pink. They were pretty, but a little plain compared to the bright red and blue fish in the neighboring tanks. The tank had no plants, but there was something white in the middle, shaped like a traffic cone. When I walked over to them, Saiki pointed to the top of the tank.

"See it?"

Following his finger, I could see something like a tadpole swimming. Its head looked like a black triangle and its tail was basically a scrap of thread. It was maybe five millimeters long. It was wriggling like mad, rising and falling in the water.

"Is that the only one?"

"Look there."

Urabe held his finger over the tank, pointing down. There were little dots that looked like cod roe stuck to the side of the white cone. Some were filled with a creamy substance. Others had a black glow, but most of them were clear.

"The ones that look black inside are about to hatch. The milky ones haven't been fertilized."

The parents swam toward the surface, ready to peck at our fingers.

"They're angry," Urabe said, apparently amused. He pointed to one of the adults and said, "That's the female." The couple took turns threatening us. Meanwhile, the tadpole, oblivious to the conflict, continued to rise and fall.

"What's this fish called?"

"Discus," Saiki and Urabe answered in unison. Urabe stared at me in disgust.

"You're kidding, right?"

"Urabe's a real wizard at discus breeding."

If I knew Saiki, he was being sarcastic, but Urabe nodded, serious as could be. His Adam's apple was huge, bulging.

"I have more discus here than anything else. It's all about numbers. The more you raise, the better the pairs. The better the pairs, the better the offspring."

I looked around the room. At least ten tanks had the same round fish inside. Some tanks had only two fish, others had too many to count.

"All the pairs are couples?"

"Yeah," Urabe nodded. "Some lay lots of eggs, others don't. But quantity doesn't necessarily mean anything. One time, I had a couple that laid eggs like you've never seen. It was crazy, but none of the eggs worked out. Then I took a closer look and it turned out they were both female."

"It's really hard to tell them apart," Saiki laughed. "The male and the female."

"Hey." Urabe's wife came up behind her husband and tugged at the back of his shirt. At some point, she must have put the baby down in a corner of the room. There were snacks and coffee on the low table by the sofa.

"Oh, this is for you—for both of you."

Saiki handed the sake bottle to Urabe's wife. She took it with a smile, then disappeared into the kitchen.

As soon as she was gone, Saiki leaned toward Urabe and whispered, "Hey, how old is she?"

Urabe grinned and asked back, "How old do you think?"

Saiki looked at me. "She can't be older than twenty," I shrugged.

"Haha. Twenty, huh?"

Urabe was enjoying himself. Saiki couldn't handle the suspense. He asked again.

"Come on. How old?"

"Yeah. Twenty."

"No way." Saiki was visibly jealous. "How'd you pull that off?"

"She was always in the shop."

"The fish shop?"

"Where else?"

We sat down and drank the coffee that Urabe's young bride had made for us. Urabe hogged the bowl of snacks. Saiki had told me he was done with tropical fish, and yet he was the only one pushing the conversation in that direction. Everything they said went over my head. I'd finished my coffee, so I got back up to peer into the colorful tanks. One tank had what looked like killifish, iridescent blue and covered with different patterns, and another had something like a small scorpion fish. In the next tank, I saw a large fish that looked like a carp with well-defined scales, so I stopped.

"Hey, is this a bonytongue?" I asked.

"So you know that one, huh?" Saiki laughed.

Urabe was all business. "That one's from the shop. Too expensive for anyone to buy, I guess. If you want it, I can give it to you real cheap."

Saiki smiled cautiously. "How cheap?"

"Well, I suppose I could go as low as eighty thousand."

I couldn't believe what I was hearing. Eighty thousand yen for a single fish. But Saiki didn't miss a beat. "Eighty? That's a damn good deal. If you're willing to go that low, you should be able to sell it in no time. It's got a great shape ..." Saiki was staring at the fish now—I had to wonder if he might pull out his wallet right then and there.

Urabe sighed.

"It's too much trouble to put an ad up. Besides, if the competition saw, they'd undersell me just for the hell of it."

I took another look at the bonytongue. Its scales flashed silver in the light. It almost looked like it was pouting. Personally, I wouldn't be willing to drop that kind of money, but it really was a beautiful fish. It fanned its fins, but its eyes stayed right where they were.

Under that tank was an even bigger one, with about thirty discus inside. They were a whole lot smaller than the couple in the other tank. They had to be babies, or maybe a little older than that. It looked like some had stripes, some had tiny spots, and others had polka dots, but they were swimming around, some coming closer, others moving farther away, so it was hard to say.

"They were all born right here."

There was a voice in my ear. It was Urabe's wife, standing next to me, admiring the fish. Urabe and Saiki had gone back to talking about fish, so she probably felt bad for me. I took a good look at her face. She wasn't wearing any makeup. Maybe that was why she looked so young.

"They have all kinds of patterns ..."

"Yeah, they do."

The neon light from the tank cast spots on her face. I could see fine veins in her cheeks.

"We still don't fully understand the relationship between genotype and phenotype. We haven't been able to confirm which genes lead to which patterns. He says that's why we need to experiment with different pairings—to see which combinations they produce."

I didn't know what to say. I guess I wasn't expecting someone so young to use that kind of language.

"You mean like Mendel? To figure out what's dominant or recessive ... Like that?"

"Yeah."

"I see. So two fish with stripes won't necessarily produce offspring with stripes ..."

"Exactly. So he's pairing the fish to observe the outcomes."

"Is he publishing his findings anywhere?"

"I bet he could, if he wanted to."

She smiled.

I thought about my sisters. Having kids completely changed their appearances. They stopped wearing makeup and bought different kinds of clothes. They changed the way they spoke. It was like they became different people. I wondered what Urabe's wife would look like if she went out with friends her own age, if she did her hair and put on makeup. She'd probably be one of those girls going around in miniskirts, the kind I tried to stay away from. She was skinny—only her breasts didn't match the rest of her body. They looked really heavy. I felt bad for her. I wanted to ask her why she'd married a man twice her age, someone who'd never even had a real job, but I thought better of it. I'd never met them before and I didn't want to offend either of them. Besides, it wasn't any of my business.

"You're twenty, right? So what year were you born?"

She opened her mouth like she was about to say something, then stopped. I started to feel guilty that we'd asked Urabe how old she was. I went back to looking at the fish. I could see a few red spirals at the bottom of the clear water. I was about to ask her what the spirals were when she whispered, "Um, do you want to have a drink?" She smelled so sweet that I had to look away. "We don't have much, but ..."

"Please, don't worry about that ... with the baby and all ..."

Before we got here, I'd imagined that the three of us were going to be doing some serious drinking. But Saiki had no idea that Urabe had a wife and kid. Things being what they were, Saiki's big bottle of sake was clearly not the right gift for the occasion. We would have been better off with a basket of fruit.

"Hey, are you talking about drinks?"

Behind me, Urabe's voice filled the room. When I turned around, Saiki was sitting with an oversized book open in his lap. I had no idea where it had come from.

"I was just wondering if we should open the bottle they brought ..." Urabe's wife was blushing.

"Yeah. Open it up," Urabe said.

He got up from the couch and walked over to the dining area. At the center of the table, there was a small tank full of red-bellied fish. Saiki's eyes were glued to the book and the pictures of tropical fish inside—it was almost like he couldn't hear us. Urabe's wife went into the kitchen. The baby was still sleeping in the corner. No crying, nothing. I could hear glasses clinking in the other room.

"Come on," I tried to get Saiki to join us. He got up with the book in his hands, then sat down at the table, across from Urabe. I took the seat next to him. Unsurprisingly, I was staring right into another discus tank. This tank was bigger than the others, with two fish inside, swimming close to one another.

"They're originally from Asia, right?"

Saiki held the book in front of Urabe, his finger on one of the pictures.

"Malaysia. Doesn't it say that?"

"How would I know? I can't read English. Oh, wait. Yeah, it says Malaysia."

"Yeah, this sounds like a lot. It's got to be freshwater, and the pH needs to stay around ..."

I couldn't keep up, so I stopped trying. Urabe's wife came out with Saiki's bottle, two little glasses, and a ceramic teacup. She set the glasses down in front of Saiki and me, put the teacup in front of her husband, then rushed back to the kitchen. I could hear the stove clicking on. Urabe uncorked the bottle and filled our glasses.

"Hey, we need chopsticks," Urabe called to his wife in the kitchen. "And more snacks. Just bring out whatever we've got." It didn't seem right to have a new mother running around like that only a month after giving birth. I thought about how I'd have to take care of my wife if she ever got pregnant. Urabe's wife came back from the kitchen, this time with two pairs of disposable wooden chopsticks and one lacquered set. "This is all we have ..." She bowed her head as she placed the disposable chopsticks in front of Saiki and me.

"No worries," I said with a wave of my hand.

"No more snacks? Damn ..." Urabe stood up, went over to a cabinet with a fish tank on top, opened it, and pulled out a plastic bag. He came back to the table, pulled a couple of tissues from a box in front of Saiki, flattened them out on the table, then dumped the bag out over them.

Dried shrimp.

"Here we go. Saiki, get your face out of that book. If you want it, it's yours. Join the conversation, though."

Once he finally looked up, Saiki saw the shrimp and jerked back. "Is that ..."

"Sure is," Urabe grinned as he picked a shrimp from the pile and put it in his mouth. I was about to grab one, but Saiki reached out to stop me.

"What?" I asked, but Saiki didn't answer. "H-Hey, Urabe . . ." Saiki's voice shook. I didn't understand. They looked like ordinary shrimp to me.

"Why are you looking at me like that? It's just dried shrimp."

"But they're . . ."

"Totally safe. I eat them all the time."

Urabe bit into another one, took a sip from his cup, then said, "Great stuff." His giant Adam's apple slid up and down.

Saiki turned to me with a serious look and said, "The shrimp . . . are for them."

"Them?"

"The fish."

"Oh yeah?" If anything, Saiki's words only piqued my interest. "I thought fish ate pellets or something." I thought back to feeding the classroom killifish when I was in grade school.

"Fish eat all kinds of things. Frozen stuff, live bait . . ."

"Live bait?"

"Yeah, crickets, worms, frogs . . . When a bonytongue gets as big as that one, it'll swallow anything. They all have their preferences, though. You have to find the right food for the right fish."

"What do you feed the discus?"

"Frozen bloodworms. Wanna see?"

"Guys," Saiki spoke up before I could. "I thought we were drinking."

"Come on, just try one. It's real good. Way healthier than most of the junk people eat."

I grabbed one and took a bite.

"These aren't roasted, are they?"

"Nope."

The smell was better than the taste. It was edible—just a little on the salty side.

"Not bad."

Saiki looked at me in disbelief. "Man, I didn't know you had it in you."

"What? It's just shrimp. It's not a cricket or anything."

"It's all fish food," Saiki said as he took a sip from his glass.

Urabe's wife came out holding a steaming plate with something flat and yellow on it. It had to be eggs. Urabe looked at the plate, then at his wife, and asked, "Did you remember to season it?"

His wife nodded.

"Tell you what ... Should we just order a pizza?"

"A pizza?"

"I'm going to the store. I'll be right back," Urabe's wife said in a small voice. She nodded at us, then left.

"What about the baby? What if she wakes up?"

Urabe shook his head and said with a mouthful of egg, "Won't happen. She never cries. I always thought having a baby would be a huge pain. I thought she'd keep me up all night, but it's been a real breeze."

"You just don't wake up," Saiki said. "You've always been like that. Remember when we went on that trip for school? We took your sleeping bag, took off your clothes, and wrote all over you with a sharpie. You still didn't wake up."

Urabe laughed.

"Yeah, that was messed up. When I got up that morning, the teacher really went off on me, but why? All I did was sleep ..."

"I bet she cries every night. You just sleep through it. Anyway, how'd you end up with this beautiful girl? She walked into the store? Then what? You said something to her? Did she come up to you?"

"Well, not exactly," Urabe said with a grin. "I'd say she came up to me, but I don't want to sound full of myself. Hey, this isn't half bad. She's a good girl, but not the best cook …"

"What difference does that make? If she's that young, right?"

Saiki looked at me and I nodded along.

"She's a real catch."

"You think? When she told me she was pregnant, I kind of freaked out. I never really thought about starting a family or anything. But to be honest, it's not that bad."

"Frankly, I'm surprised her parents gave you their blessing. It's not like you have a job or anything."

I grabbed a chunk of egg with my chopsticks and put it into my mouth. Beyond the sugar and soy sauce, I thought I could pick up on some sesame oil. In no time, Urabe had poured another full cup of sake for himself.

"So what if I don't have a job? It's all about money, and I've never had any problems on that front. Technically, I get a salary anyway. From my dad's company."

"Screw that."

"Taxes, man. It's the least I can do to help out with the family business."

I didn't want to come home drunk. I didn't want to show up like that, then have the usual talk with my wife. I listened to Urabe and Saiki go back and forth. I occasionally brought my glass up to my mouth, but never had more than a sip.

Urabe looked at my glass, then at me. "Not much of a drinker, huh?"

"Oh, he's a real lightweight," Saiki answered for me. I just nodded as if I wasn't bothered.

"That right? He's got the face of a drinker," Urabe said. I stroked my cheek. "What do you think you're gonna feel?" Urabe cackled as he topped off his drink and Saiki's.

"Your wife said you're researching discus genetics?"

"Well, I'd hardly call it research. Just picking mates, observing the results."

"So a lot of thought goes into pairing them?"

Urabe took a second to think. Saiki had the same book out again. He was propping up his cheek with one hand and poking at the pages with the other.

"Maybe. In a way, there's a lot of intention behind it. At the same time, it's pretty intuitive."

"It's too hard to explain," Saiki added, even though he was barely listening.

"It's the same for people, though." Urabe stood up and walked over to the tank with his cup in his hand. "We meet at school, or work, or maybe a store. Wherever it is, there's just a random group of individuals, right? Within that group, you find your mate. If you were in a different group, you'd end up with a different mate, right? But we never dwell on that. We live our lives in the groups we have—in our cities, our countries, even though we didn't choose them. Know what I mean? We like to tell ourselves it's love, that we're choosing our own partners. But in reality, we're just playing the cards we've been dealt."

When Urabe got close enough to the tank, the fish inside gathered together and came toward him.

"I bet they're hungry."

"They just ate," Urabe said as he came back to the table. His cup was empty again. "Hey, I almost forgot. I've got a story to tell you. It's a sad one."

"No sad stories, thanks," Saiki replied as he flipped through the book.

"Fine, a funny story . . . Back when the shop was still open, there were days when I'd go back into the stockroom and everything would be all over the place. Bags of fish food I had up on the shelves would be down on the floor, ripped open and half-eaten."

"Oh yeah?" Saiki's eyes didn't leave the book.

Urabe just kept going. "At first, I had no idea what was happening ..."

I'd only had a sip or two, but Urabe filled my glass to the top. I watched the liquor dribble down the side, then I reached for another shrimp. Once I'd had one, I found myself wanting more. Saiki wasn't saying anything, so I jumped in. "Well?" Urabe stuck out the tip of his white tongue, licked at the corner of his mouth, then went on.

"I kept putting everything back, but the same thing happened the next day, and the day after that. Then one night, I heard a crash. I went downstairs to see what it was. I could hear rustling in the stockroom, and the door was open ..."

"You left it unlocked?" Saiki glanced up at Urabe with only his eyes.

"Why shouldn't I? It's just a little room for storing fish food." Urabe took another bite of egg. "Anyway, I stood there for a second, wondering if I should go in. I guess I felt like I had to. I grabbed the steel bar that had the shutter key on it and burst in."

"What was it?" Saiki asked, putting the book down.

Urabe locked eyes with Saiki, then me. He smirked, then continued. "It was a girl, in her underwear."

"Huh?"

"Yeah. This grade-school girl, staring at me, chewing on something. Her eyes were glowing. It was like she was looking right through me."

"And she was in her underwear?"

"Yeah. A sheer slip over white cotton underwear. When I threw open the door, she didn't even flinch. She was just looking at me. Then I turned the light on and saw what she was eating. Dried shrimp. Just like these."

I put another one in my mouth and bit into the crunchy shell.

"We were just standing there, so I asked her something and she answered me. I couldn't believe it."

"Wait, what did you think she was gonna do?"

"No, you had to see her. She looked like one of those kids, you know? Like she was mute or something. She had that kind of look. She wasn't much of a talker, but we could communicate, so I asked her what was going on. She told me she lived in the neighborhood. She didn't have any money. No food, either. Her mom worked nights, so she was always home alone with nothing to eat. That's why she snuck in."

"But why there?"

"I guess she came by earlier in the day, when the shop was open. It sounded like she'd set her sights on one of the fish. Crazy, right? Think about it. This little girl outside my shop, staring at these exotic fish swimming around in the tanks, salivating. Anyway, yeah, that was maybe six or seven years ago."

"Come on, I'm not buying it. There's a convenience store right down the street. She could—"

"She tried," Urabe said with a smile. "She'd already been caught stealing there." Urabe drank everything in his cup, filled it, and took another gulp. "She was poor. It was just her and her mom. I felt bad, so I gave her a bag of shrimp. She bowed at me a bunch of times, then ran off. She probably waited for her mom to get back and split it with her. Anyway, shrimp's good for you. Lots of protein."

"Wait a second," Saiki reached for the bottle and poured himself another round. "If you knew that, why didn't you give her an actual meal? Or, I don't know, money? Why would you send her home with fish food? Isn't that kinda messed up?"

"Hey, if I gave her money, she'd definitely come back for more. Wouldn't that be worse?"

"She came back anyway, right?"

"Well, yeah. She showed up a few days later, in normal clothes, during business hours. I didn't give her anything that time. There were customers around. After that, she started coming to the stockroom at night. Whenever I saw her, I'd give her another bag of shrimp. She was probably coming once a month or so . . ."

"That's really messed up."

"It's funny—that's what it is. I only gave her fish food, but she kept coming back."

"Then she must have been in real trouble when you closed shop for good."

"I dunno."

The door opened and Urabe's wife came in carrying some large plastic bags. "Welcome back," I said. She looked up, apparently surprised, and said, "Thanks."

She let go of the bags digging into her arms and spread everything out on the table.

Urabe reached for a pack of fried chicken. "You didn't have them heated at the store?"

"You can eat it cold," I said without thinking.

Urabe's wife took the pack of chicken and headed silently into the kitchen. I could hear the microwave start. In the meantime, Urabe tore into a pack of pickles, plucked out a piece of eggplant, and stuck it in his mouth.

I looked at all the food Urabe's wife had brought back. Dried squid, peanuts, takoyaki, and a few other snacks. My eyes landed on a bag of rice crackers.

"Help yourself," Urabe said. I opened the bag and put one in my mouth. The soy flavor was so strong that I was forced to wash it down with sake. Urabe saw me and said, "Yeah, that's the spirit." As soon as I set my glass down, he filled it. There was a loud pop in the other room. Urabe's wife ran into the kitchen to open the microwave. Saiki opened the book again and held it up so Urabe could see.

"Hey, where'd this fin come from? The parents?"

"Well, it's some kind of a mutation."

"Out in the wild?"

"It's not like mutations don't happen in the wild."

Urabe's wife came out with a few pieces of fried chicken on a plate, looked at me, and smiled. I smiled back, then looked down at the chicken. All the pieces had lost their shape.

"Was his wife representing the family?"

"No." Saiki paused for a while on the other end of the line. "His dad was. She wasn't even at the service. I looked for her, but ..."

"Maybe she was at home with the baby?"

Saiki took a few seconds to answer. "It looks like they weren't actually married."

"Wait, you mean the baby wasn't ..."

"No, it was Urabe's. I wanted to know more, but I couldn't exactly ask anybody about it ..."

I remembered her slim body and large breasts. The baby asleep in my arms, warm and damp.

"What happened to Urabe, though? Was he sick?"

"I guess we'll never know," Saiki said with a strange finality.

Neither of us said anything for a while. Then Saiki sighed into the receiver. "I can't take funerals like this. We were the same age, you know?"

"What happened to all his fish?"

"I guess his dad called a pro to see what he could sell, but it sounds like Urabe was dead for a few days before anyone knew anything. By that time, most of the fish were beyond saving."

"What about the discus?"

"Who knows. He had so many, too. His dad asked me to take whatever I wanted, but ... I dunno, I couldn't do it."

It occurred to me that I should take a pair—a male and a female.

"Don't do it. I know Urabe made it look easy, but they're tricky fish. Breeding them is a real pain in the ass. You've never even changed a tank, have you? They eat bugs, too. Your wife would hate that."

That night, my wife had gone to bed an hour or two before me. When I got into bed, she was crying. She got her period again. "This isn't working. We need to know what the problem is. We need to get your sperm tested ..."

"Consider it done," I said as I got under the blankets. My cheeks were still warm from the beer I'd had. My wife turned away from me. I reached out and stroked her back. Even under the blanket, her back felt hard and bony. After a couple of minutes, I couldn't hear her crying anymore. I pulled the blanket up to my neck.

How did Urabe die?

I thought about the newly hatched discus I'd seen at his house. I shut my eyes and I could see it in my mind, shaking its ribbony tail, rising and falling in the water. I knew what Saiki was saying, but I still wanted a pair for myself. I just wanted to see what kind of offspring they'd have.

The little discus suddenly stopped moving its tail and floated to the surface. I opened my eyes. My wife was looking at me. Her eyes were wide open, glowing like pools of light.

THE LAST OF THE WEASELS

WE DIDN'T VISIT MY WIFE'S FAMILY FOR NEW YEAR'S.
"It's fine," she said, shrugging her shoulders. "I'll go on my own
when I have the time. It's not that far away." From time to time,
she did go back home without me. For my part, I saw no real reason to see my wife's parents or my sister-in-law's family. "I'll just
ask Mom to give the kids a little something from us." "Sounds
good—if you're sure."

The holidays came and went. I'd already been back at work
for a while by the time I got a New Year's card from Saiki with
a picture of the year's zodiac animal printed on the front. It had
a short message scribbled in ballpoint pen:

> *Moved house. Holidays were hectic. Got married. Bride*
> *is thirty-two.*

It was just like Saiki to mention her age. Thirty-two meant that
she was about ten years his junior. His new house was maybe an
hour's drive from town, just shy of the Chugoku Mountains, in
an area where many of the residents did a little farming on the
side. For Saiki to get married and move into a new home like that
was a big change. I figured I ought to give him a call.

"Hey there," Saiki said loudly as he picked up. "How have
you been?"

"I just got your card. Thought I should call and say congrats. So—you're married now?"

"I know, I know. I'm a new man. This house is another story, though. It's been here for fifty years, so we had to do some serious renovation." He sounded a little drunk. "Sorry to drop that on you in a card. I told some people from work, but failed to share the big news with my closest friends."

Saiki worked at home. He spoke as if his tongue was getting in the way. I could hear a clamor of voices behind him.

"You having a get-together or something?"

"No, nothing that fancy. We're way out in the country here. People just swing by. I grew up in the city, so this is all strange to me. The old guys from around the neighborhood show up night after night, raring to drink. They've got nothing but time. Anyway, I messed up ... I messed everything up."

I messed up, he said, but he sounded overjoyed. He must've had a lot to drink.

"But you're married now. That's cause for celebration, right?"

"Well, yeah. Getting married for the first time, after forty, is a little ... I don't know. It feels kind of weird. Not in a bad way, though. What about you? How's the wife holding up? She doing okay?"

"Yeah." She actually hadn't been great. Her work was draining, but—even more than that—I felt like not getting pregnant was really weighing on her. "She's been good, thanks for asking. Well, get-together or not, I don't want to keep you. Just wanted to call and say congrats."

One day not long before that, right when I got home, my wife rushed to meet me at the door and brought the sweet smell of rice with her.

"Uh, I'm home."

"Hey ..." The look on her face was weirdly serious. I didn't know what was going on, so I mirrored her expression. "What is it?" "Well, um ..." My wife wasn't usually one to beat around the bush. She was still in her office clothes, so she couldn't have been home for very long. There was something round in her hand. It was semitransparent white plastic, maybe two inches in diameter. It looked like one of those covered containers for prescription creams that you get from the dermatologist.

"Have you been, um, handling things ... yourself?"

"Handling things?" I stared at my wife, confused. "What things?"

"How can I put it ..." My wife looked down at the container in her hand, then broke into a faint smile. "I mean, do you ever, um ... You know ..." I was shocked by the look she was giving me.

"Oh, you mean ... Use my hand and stuff to ... Do I do *that*?"

"Yeah." She nodded. I had no idea what to say. My face must've been bright red.

"No, never, not since we got married ..." That was the truth. It's not like I was in my teens or twenties. As a man in his forties with a wife the same age, watching her desperately staring at calendars and BBT charts month after month, it really was the last thing on my mind. At this age, I bet even Saiki doesn't do that anymore—and he had enough energy to marry someone ten years younger.

"Why would you ask me ..."

"Oh, I'm not accusing you of anything." The smile faded from her lips. Her forehead was oily, but her cheeks were still powdered. Looking at her feet, she had only one stocking on. She must have been in a hurry to talk.

"What's going on?"

"Um, I hate to ask, I really do," my wife said, speaking much quicker now. "But I want you to ejaculate into this."

She held up the container.

"Sorry, what?" My jaw dropped. "For a test or something? To see if ..."

"Uh-huh." Her smile returned as she nodded. "If I can get it to the gynecologist within the next twenty-four hours, they can run the test for us. I stopped by, after work ..."

I took the container. It was warm from her hand. "You want it tonight?"

"Tomorrow morning is best. The fresher the better ... But now's fine, too ..."

That explains why she was in such a hurry. I'm not as young as I used to be. What if I couldn't perform on command? She wanted to make sure I had a few options. After all, we'd had a couple of peak fertility nights that we'd missed because I couldn't do my part, and that always ended with both of us feeling utterly exhausted.

"I know it's a lot to ask ... I'll sleep in the other room tonight. It would be hard to do with me around, right?"

"It doesn't bother me any." All of a sudden, I couldn't keep myself from laughing. It was a real laugh. The whole thing was just too funny. My wife started laughing, too. It felt like it'd been years since we'd really laughed together. Until I'd opened the front door that evening, there was no way I could have imagined we'd find ourselves laughing at a time like this.

We ate dinner and took our baths. When my wife was ready to go to bed, she said, "Just make sure you get all of it in there." She waited for me to nod. "No wiping, okay? Not until you're done." "Got it."

When spring came, I got a phone call from Saiki. I had the day off and my wife was out. She wasn't trying to make up for missing New Year's, but she took a trip home. As soon as I picked up, Saiki asked me if I knew anything about weasels.

"Weasels?"

I had to make sure I was hearing him right.

"Yeah, I've got weasels, and they're a real problem. The whole situation is bumming me out. There's this hag down the street ..."

"Hag?"

"Yeah, she's a real piece of work. It's a nightmare over here. I mean, you should see my wife's arms. They're swollen and bright red ..."

"Her arms?" I had no idea what Saiki was trying to say. He stopped to take a swig of something. It was the middle of the day—too early to be drinking, I thought, but who knows what people who work at home get up to in the middle of the afternoon.

"Damn weasels. They're up above us, making all this noise ... Then there's the bugs. I don't know if they're fleas or ticks, but they're all over the place. My wife's arms are looking real bad ... And let me tell you, weasel crap stinks like hell. I'm at the end of my rope. It was a big mistake coming here." The voice on the other end of the line sounded pitiful—nothing like the Saiki I knew.

"Call an exterminator," I said, but it wasn't that easy, not according to Saiki.

He tried a local exterminator, but the guy wasn't much help. "I can put down a trap, if you want," he said timidly, "but weasels can be tricky." Saiki had him go into the attic. "The guy said he found shit, clumps of fur, and a den made out of chewed-up insulation we'd just installed. He told me he put the trap right there. The next day, we caught one. *The next day*. At that point, all I could think was that the guy had to be messing with me. Know what I mean?"

When the exterminator came back, he told Saiki that the one in the trap was a baby. It had golden fur, and its body was longer and thinner than Saiki had imagined. "I thought it was going to look like a weird dog or something, but it didn't look anything like that. It was a lot longer and skinnier."

The exterminator was sure that the weasel they'd caught wasn't there alone. He told Saiki that they'd better set another trap or the first one would have been for nothing—and he was right. They caught another one before the week was up—and another the day after that. At that point, the exterminator told Saiki it'd be cheaper if he bought his own trap. So that's what Saiki and his wife did. Sometimes they'd find weasels in the trap a few days in a row. Other times, a week or two would pass and they'd feel like the ordeal was finally over—until another one got caught.

"It sounds like the exterminator was a nice guy. You already made your money back off the trap."

Saiki said he drove the weasels he'd caught into the mountains, maybe fifteen miles away.

"To the mountains? If you're going to do that, what's the point?"

"Well, it's not like an animal shelter's gonna take a wild weasel off your hands. The mountains are miles away. There's no way they're going to make it back from that distance. What would you do? Kill them?" I was quiet for a little while, then said, "No way."

"Weasels are apparently really, really stupid. You lay a trap and they'll walk right into it, over and over." No matter how hard you try to get rid of them, they keep coming back. Saiki said he felt like he'd already caught every weasel in the area—but new ones kept getting trapped. The exterminator told Saiki that they weren't living in the house. They had to be coming in from somewhere, then getting caught in the trap or finding their way out again. In other words, they had to find the hole—wherever it was—and patch it. If they didn't, the weasels were never going to stop coming.

"I swear I'm gonna lose it. Forget about 'toys in the attic,' weasels are way worse ..."

"But all you've got to do is find the hole, right?"

Saiki took a couple of gulps of whatever he was drinking. The house he'd bought was a fifty-year-old Japanese-style home with a tiled roof, so he'd had the place renovated as soon as he got it. He put in insulation, replaced the steep stairs, added handrails, made the floors level, and even converted a few of the tatami rooms. The whole process was cheaper than buying a new house, but it still set him back. At the time, he didn't know about the weasels, so he didn't bother filling in the gaps under the floor, in the walls, or under the roof. When you think about it, Japanese homes are full of holes. "I can't do anything about them now. I'd have to build the whole thing over. It would have been better if I'd just built a new place from scratch, but it's too late for that now. At this point, I don't have the money to start over. Listen, when you think about buying a house, give it some real thought, okay? Once the weasels show up, you're done for. This never would have happened if we'd moved into one of those boxy manufactured houses. Those things are airtight. A fifty-year-old house ... What the hell was I thinking?"

It sounded too strange to me. "So the last owner never had a weasel problem?" Saiki took one more swig of his drink, then went on, raising his voice in anger.

"Exactly. That's what really pisses me off. It's what I was saying about that hag next door ... Well, we're out here in the middle of nowhere, so she doesn't really live that close. Anyway, the wife was having a little chat with her ..." Did Saiki just call his new bride "the wife"? "And when she starts, you know, complaining about the weasels, our dear neighbor was like, 'So they're back ... They were a real problem for the previous family.' Up to that point, she acted like she didn't know a thing. Why didn't she say anything about the weasels when we were remodeling? Then the weasels show up, and suddenly she has tons of advice. 'Those weasels can be a real handful. That's what the last owner said ...' Unbelievable, right?"

"So she doesn't have any weasels in her place?"

"Hell no." Saiki exhaled deeply. "Never has. And her house is older than mine, with even more holes."

"I wonder why," I said, carefully sipping my tea so I didn't make a sound. It was an herbal tea that my wife had ordered for us. It had a strong smell and a bitter edge.

"You'd have to take that up with the weasels. I'm sure they've got their own preferences, not that we humans would ever understand. Anyway, her house is apparently weasel-free," Saiki said, fuming with indignation. "The same goes for every home in the neighborhood, except for mine."

"So what did the person who used to live there do?"

"No idea. All I know is that they had the same problem. That hag down the street didn't know much, either. She just smiled with all her fake teeth and mumbled something about how they vanished at some point."

"That doesn't sound good. What are you going to do?"

"Well, the wife's been doing some digging online ... Turns out there's no easy fix for a weasel problem. And you wouldn't believe what it's been costing me in gas. This old guy in the neighborhood lets me borrow his mini-truck as long as I fill the tank when I bring it back, but I swear the greedy bastard leaves the thing as empty as he can on purpose. When I show up, he looks me in the eye and says, 'I figured you'd be coming back pretty soon.' Who says people in the country are simple? It's bullshit. They're all the same as that hag. And the place is full of old men with nothing but time on their hands. Whenever we're home, these guys show up with big bottles of booze, saying *drink, drink.* All winter, they came by with boar and deer meat, urging my wife to make a stew or slice it up thin and roast it. We're the youngest couple in the neighborhood—and newcomers on top of that. The wife never really puts her foot down, either. In no time, the whole house is swarming with old guys getting wasted. I'm telling you, the countryside is no picnic."

"So the weasels aren't a problem when people come over?"

"They only show up in certain parts of the house. Probably because of how the attic was built. The dining room is safe. But the wife's got sensitive skin. You should see her arms. It's not like that for me. Anyway ..."

"Hey, don't worry about it. If I figure something out, I'll let you know."

"There's nothing to figure out. We're going to live out the rest of our days among the weasels, way out here in the middle of nowhere." Saiki sounded like he was about to cry. He took another swig of his drink and gathered himself.

"Hey, we're going to do boar stew one last time. Why don't you and your wife come out?"

"One last time?"

"It's a winter thing. Hunting season's over."

"Would we be eating with the usual crowd from the neighborhood?"

Saiki laughed on the other end of the line.

"No, no. Just us. Those old guys are too much. Besides, they've already had boar stew at our place a few times—and given it their seal of approval. We secretly got our hands on some good boar loin of our own. It's in the freezer now, so there's no rush, but why don't you two come up sometime soon?"

I told him I'd check with my wife when she got home, then we got off the phone. I assumed she wouldn't be interested, but when she came back that evening—her arms heavy with all kinds of bags—I asked her and she said she'd be happy to go.

"Boar stew is such a luxury these days." She really did look happy.

"Wait, you've had boar before?"

My wife just giggled as she took various types of food out of the bags, then put them in the fridge. Pickled vegetables and a few other side dishes from my mother-in-law, by the looks of it.

"I grew up in the country ... But it's been years." At a minimum, I was pretty sure she hadn't eaten boar since we got married. It wasn't something I'd ever had before.

"What's it like?"

"Well, it's not like pork ... It's really soft. You'll like it. At our house, we'd have it with soy dashi and a hint of miso. It's best if it's not too sweet. I wonder what Saiki's wife is like. Is she young?"

"He says she's thirty-two."

"Oh, wow."

We parked just outside Saiki's new home, on a large property with plenty of space and a few trees: a white plum, a magnolia, and some kind of tall evergreen.

"Hey, you guys made it," Saiki said as he came out to greet us. He must have heard us pulling up.

As I congratulated Saiki again on his marriage, he broke into a grin, turned to my wife, and said, "Look who it is! It's been a long time." My wife handed him the box of sweets she'd brought as a gift.

"Yeah, it's been a while. Congratulations. And thanks for having us. Is your wife inside?"

"She's in the kitchen," Saiki said, still grinning. "I think you'll like her cooking."

He looked like he'd put on a little weight.

"I can see it agrees with you just fine."

"Hey," Saiki's grin was even bigger now. "At this age, you need a little extra padding."

"Look at this beautiful house. This is a nice space, too. Hey, what's that tall tree called?"

"It's some kind of willow. We've got a persimmon tree out back, but the fruit's apparently bitter."

"You've got a plum tree, too."

"Yeah. This is how the old owners had it. Considering all the space, we really don't have much in terms of trees. I'd like to change that, but more trees would mean more yard work, right?"

I went over to the plum tree. It had been a bad year for plums all around. I'm pretty sure they were late to bloom, too. Saiki's plum blossoms looked tiny. There weren't many of them, either. Hoping they'd at least smell nice, I brought my nose close, but instead of the modest scent of blossoms all I could smell was the tree gathering its energy for budding.

"Are those wild cherries?" my wife muttered, almost too quiet to hear, looking up at the mountains beyond Saiki's house. The mountains were still mostly gray-brown, but there was green in places and a few patches of white here and there. "Plums and cherries at the same time?"

"Cherry trees bloom earlier in the mountains," I said as Saiki showed us in. From the outside, his house was the picture of the traditional Japanese home, but as soon as we stepped inside I could tell he'd made some big changes.

The entryway was tiled and the step up into the house was low.

"I'm only going to get older. I made a few changes with the future in mind. Anyway, come on in." When I took off my shoes and stepped inside, I caught the smell of sweet miso from the kitchen.

"It smells great." My wife took off her coat and threw it over one arm as she wiggled her nose.

"Makes me so happy to hear it. I know you're going to love the stew. Oh, you can hang your coat right here."

"Hold on." A woman's voice came from inside. "I'll get some hangers." Maybe I was imagining things, but it looked like my wife was adjusting her posture. Rolling back her right shoulder, then the left, straightening out to her full height. The woman who appeared from the kitchen had bushy eyebrows, with her knees hidden by a long skirt and her shoulders hunched inside a turtleneck sweater. Her swollen arms were covered.

"Hi, it's nice to meet you." Saiki's wife bowed, then handed us a pair of wire hangers, the kind they have at the cleaners.

"This is Yoko," Saiki said with an unaffected smile. She seemed much more down-to-earth than I'd expected. My wife's wool coat was swaying on the hanger, so she grabbed it by the shoulders for a moment, then slowly let go. Once she was sure that Yoko had gone inside, my wife leaned closer and whispered in my ear. "He said she was thirty-two, right?"

"I'm pretty sure, yeah."

"Right?" my wife said. "Most women in their early thirties still think of themselves as young, but . . ." She gave me a serious sort of look. "She seems pretty relaxed."

"Yeah, definitely," I said, nodding back.

The kitchen had plenty of space, and my wife gasped with envy the second she saw it. Yoko turned around and smiled.

"There's lots of room, but it's really old-fashioned."

"But you've got four burners . . . and all these cabinets."

"Yeah. But after I'm done using something and put it away, the next time I go looking for it, I can never find it. I think I've lost at least a couple of drop lids."

Yoko gathered her hair and held it up with a rhinestone clip, then started chopping water celery.

"Is there anything I can do to help?" my wife asked.

"Not a chance!" Saiki shouted. "Have a seat, relax. Remind me, do you drink?" Saiki pulled out a chair for my wife and I sat down next to her. Their dining table was easily big enough to seat eight.

"She can drink more than I can."

"That's true. My husband's a lightweight, you know."

"But he hardly ever drinks, so it works out perfectly. He was always looking out for me when I was getting wasted. Okay, he'll drive tonight. You should drink."

Saiki pulled a lightly frosted glass decanter out of the fridge. There were some thin ceramic sake cups already out on the table.

"Cold sake. Boar warms the body, so it goes best with a cold drink. Or would you rather start with a beer?"

"No, sake sounds great. What about your wife? Yoko-san, are you going to drink?"

My wife quickly crossed her legs. The only thing between our feet and the wooden floor was an electric carpet. Neither of our hosts offered us slippers. There was a portable burner set up at the center of the table.

"Well, maybe a little. Just a little." Yoko's entire body rose and fell as she sliced the scallions and dumped them into a green plastic colander. Her thick socks seemed to lift off the floor with every chop. Next to the thin scallions were colanders full of mushrooms: shiitake, maitake, and enoki. There was a large earthen pot on the burner. Saiki grabbed a plastic bottle of oolong tea from the fridge and handed it to me, then set down a tall chilled glass in front of me.

"Well, let's get started. Yoko, how's it coming?"

"Hold on, before that …"

Yoko quickly washed her hands, then wiped them with a towel as she opened the fridge. She grabbed bowl after bowl—braised greens, burdock root, thinly sliced turnip with salmon roe—and handed them to Saiki, who commented on the contents of each bowl with a smile, "Looks great!" or "Hey, what's this?" I leaned over and whispered in my wife's ear. "Look at these lovebirds." She snorted with delight.

"Go ahead and start drinking. Honey, can you put the pot on?"

"Okay, here we go." Yoko handed Saiki a pair of oven mitts with funny pig faces on them. Saiki slipped them on, picked up the pot, then set it down on the burner.

My wife, who was sitting right in front of the burner knob, turned to Yoko at the fridge. "Should I turn it on?"

"Yes please!" Yoko practically sang. "I'll put it on high for now," my wife said as she twisted the knob. Yoko took a large plate out of the fridge, removed the plastic wrap, then handed it to her husband. Saiki held the plate so we could see.

"This is boar loin. First you freeze it, then you shave it into thin slices."

"Wow, it's so red." The color was halfway between red and maroon. Around the edge was a white layer of fat. The plate was covered in thin slices of meat.

"It's pretty."

"Is this your first time having boar?" Saiki asked my wife.

"It is …" she said with a smile. I thought that was funny, but I said, "It's my first time, too, of course."

Saiki poured cold sake into my wife's cup, Yoko's, then his own. Yoko picked up the bottle of tea and filled my glass.

"Well, here's to seeing each other again after all this time ..."

"No, no. Here's to the two of you—and your new home together."

"Yeah, okay," Saiki said with uncharacteristic bashfulness. Yoko looked at me and smiled. There were stray hairs at the ends of her droopy eyebrows. Apparently she wasn't so invested in her appearance.

"Okay, here's to that. Cheers."

Yoko lifted the lid off the pot with a dish towel. The sweet smell of miso rose from the pot together with the steam. I could see radish and carrots simmering. Yoko used a pair of long chopsticks to pick up the boar meat—one slice at a time—and place it in the light-brown soup. As we ate the dishes that Yoko had set out, we drank sake (tea for me) and talked about how Saiki and Yoko had met. We talked about the old days, when Saiki and I were in school.

"The meat looks ready." As soon as Yoko said the words, we reached in with our chopsticks. The layer of fat had shrunk. The meat tasted great with the still-hard water celery and scallions that had been added just as the broth came to a boil. My wife had a mouthful of the soup, then said, "It's so sweet." "Wild boar fat is pretty sweet," Yoko replied. My wife shot me a look and smiled a little. I turned to Yoko and said, "What a unique flavor." Despite the overwhelming sweetness, it really didn't taste bad.

I was full before long, so I put my chopsticks down even though there was plenty of meat left. My wife was still going strong and Yoko kept adding more meat to the pot. Saiki picked at the pickles as he drank his sake.

"By the way, what happened with the weasels?"

"The weasels ..." He made a face as if the cold sake he'd just swallowed had scalded his throat.

"They're still around. We bagged two more last week. Well, 'bagged' makes it sound like we wanted to ..."

"We haven't even been using bait and they're still getting caught," Yoko added, stirring the pot with the long chopsticks to make sure the meat didn't stick.

"No bait? So what's drawing them in?"

"The smell, probably. I bet it smells like a potential mate or something. Every time a weasel gets caught, it smells awful. It's disgusting to us, but maybe the other weasels are actually drawn to it."

My wife lifted her face. "Boar meat doesn't have any smell at all, does it?"

"You're right. These days, the pork you buy at the supermarket has more of a smell to it."

My wife's cheeks were looking a little rosy. Yoko had said she'd only have a little to drink, but she'd put away at least a few cups. Whenever the women emptied their cups, Saiki poured them another round without missing a beat. The three of them were looking flushed as the drinks started to take effect, and I felt a little left out. The boar meat really did warm the body, and I could feel my cheeks getting a little pink even though I hadn't been drinking.

"So the battle for the attic hasn't ended yet ..."

"With weasels, it's no battle. It's a war of attrition. According to the woman next door, it took years for the previous owners to get rid of their unwanted guests. It's not something that ends after a year or two. We've got to be patient." I couldn't tell if Saiki didn't want to say it in front of Yoko, or if he felt like he couldn't with my wife there, but he didn't call the neighbor a "hag" this time. My wife took another slice of meat with her chopsticks, then picked out some broth-soaked mushrooms and put them in her bowl. Her lips glistened with boar fat where her lipstick used to be. The tip of Yoko's nose was bright red as she stirred the pot. A swirl of gray-brown scum clung to the edge of the pot. A piece of enoki had tangled itself around one of Yoko's long chopsticks.

My wife laid her chopsticks down across her bowl with a clink. She downed the rest of the sake in her cup and practically groaned, "God, what a meal. That was amazing. Saiki-san, you must be so happy to have a wife who can cook like this." She smiled at Saiki and his red face got even redder. For a second, he looked like he was about to say something, but he held back.

"I could never make boar like this—not in a million years. Where's the sweetness come from? Mirin and sugar?"

"Mhm. It's water and sake, half and half. Bring it to a boil and add mirin and sugar ... Katsuo is overkill, so I go with konbu. Then I finish it off with a little barley miso."

"Unfortunately, I'll never have the chance to make it." My wife tapped her bright-red cheeks so loud that I could hear it, then grabbed my glass and had a mouthful of tea. She set the glass down on the table and said, "We had weasels once—when I was a kid." Hngh, Saiki groaned. I didn't know what to say, either. Yoko stood up, got a fresh glass for my wife, and filled it with tea.

"You had weasels?"

"Uh-huh. Thanks for the tea. I'll turn off the heat." My wife twisted the knob, her rose-colored fingernails moving in a small circle.

"When was that?" Saiki asked, pouring some sake for himself and his wife. Yoko practically tossed the chopsticks into the pot, fell back into her chair, then looked at my wife, resting her cheek in her palm. She had to be really drunk. Only a moment or two ago, she'd been stirring the pot attentively, but now her eyes looked red and bleary.

"This was when I was a kid, so it had to be thirty years ago. At least that. Anyway, this family of weasels started living in our attic." My wife took a gulp of tea. "At night, they made so much noise you'd think they were fighting. When it started, we thought they were rats, but at some point this liquid started dripping down over the tokonoma ... from the ceiling. It got all over what we had hanging up. The smell was horrible. Then I got this bad rash. So my parents said it couldn't be rats. It had to be weasels."

"Sounds just like us, doesn't it?" Saiki said to his wife. "Sure does," Yoko muttered, still resting her cheek in her palm. She reached for her cup with her other hand. While it wasn't any of my business, I couldn't help but think she should probably call it quits for the night. Saiki didn't even seem to notice; his glowing eyes were fixed on my wife. "Then what? What happened after that?"

"Well ..." My wife smiled. "I was a kid, so all I did was watch, but my dad and my grandpa went into the attic with a trap."

"Same as us ... Then what?"

"A little later, we caught one—an adult." My wife grabbed a slice of turnip from the bowl in front of her and put it in her mouth. A single salmon egg fell off the turnip and landed on the table. "My grandma said, 'Great, we got one of the parents.' I remember when I saw its face. I thought it was kinda cute. Those little ears and that flat snout ... It was covered in golden fur, and it had tiny little legs ... It kept moving, wriggling around inside this tiny cage. It didn't look like an adult, at least not to me. It was too cute. And it was looking at me with these beady black eyes. The weasel was moving around like crazy, but its eyes stayed on me the whole time."

"Yeah, that sounds right." Even Saiki seemed to be feeling the effects of the alcohol. Yoko could hardly keep her eyes open. She looked like she was about to fall asleep. A column of steam was still rising from the pot. I got up and cracked a window. A gust of crisp, cool air blew in. I caught the fragrance of the white plum that I hadn't been able to smell when we first arrived. I had no idea why, but my wife's voice sounded strangely high.

"I just wanted to let it go free, or maybe keep it as a pet. Not that I could, obviously. I had this rash all over my body. The whole time, the weasel kept staring at me—and it smelled so bad. When I asked my parents what they were going to do, they said they'd get rid of it, then told me to go play somewhere. My mom said they were going to throw it in the river. I felt bad, but I thought the weasel would survive. Like it would find its way downstream to safety. That didn't bother me too much, so I told my mom I'd stay there."

Saiki nodded along. I pictured my in-laws' faces. Both of them had always looked so kind and harmless, like they couldn't bring themselves to kill a fly. Thirty years ago, they would have been younger than my wife and I are now.

I just couldn't picture them drowning a weasel.

"Meanwhile, my grandparents went and got this big trash can. It was huge. I know I was only a kid at the time, but I could have fit inside it, no problem. It was a bright shade of blue. Anyway, they were carrying this trash can over—slowly. My dad asked them what they were doing. When they set it down, I could hear water sloshing around. When I looked inside, it was maybe half full of water. Then my grandpa walked off. My grandma looked at me and told me to go play somewhere. I told her I was staying right there. She told me that was okay, if that was what I wanted, then went after my grandpa. A little while later, they came back, both of them carrying buckets of water. They dumped the water into the trash can. My parents stood there like they were frozen. My mom asked my dad something. He just cocked his head and said nothing. My grandparents made a few more trips, dumping buckets of water into the trash can until it was full." My wife took another sip of her tea. "That whole time, the weasel never stopped circling around the cage."

Saiki looked stunned. Yoko looked like she was sleeping, but she suddenly opened her eyes and got up to shut the window that I'd just opened. When she sat down again, she put her cheek back in her palm, then closed her eyes.

"My grandpa picked up the cage with the weasel still inside. At some point it must have peed, and urine was trickling from the bottom of the cage onto the ground. My grandpa carried the cage over to the trash can and dunked it in the water. I don't know why, but the metal cage was floating to the surface, so my grandpa held it down, pushing it deeper into the water. When he did, I heard the most horrible sound." "Sound?" someone said in a low voice. My wife glanced at me, then faced the pot again, almost like she was talking to it. Saiki was staring at my wife, his mouth still hanging open.

"It was this series of piercing shrieks. I'd never heard anything like it before—and I haven't heard it since, not once. The weasel was screaming with everything it had." At some point, my wife said, the cage stopped floating and sank to the bottom. There was a little splosh as its face sank under the water. The last she saw the weasel's face, its mouth was open and its eyes were closed. For a while, little bubbles rose furiously to the surface. The sound never stopped. "I can still hear it now. When I looked at my mom, she was crying. My grandparents had their hands together in prayer. My dad was standing with his hands on his hips, his shoulders drooping. Once the screaming and the bubbles had stopped, my dad asked my grandpa what he was thinking, doing that right in front of the house." The color suddenly returned to Saiki's face. He reached for the bottle of tea next to me, so I handed it to him. Without really getting up, Saiki grabbed a couple of glasses and filled them with tea, setting one in front of himself and the other in front of Yoko. He took a sip. My wife was still staring at the pot. It was thick and mass-manufactured, with chunky plum blossoms drawn in white glaze against a light-brown background.

"My grandma told my dad that it was the mother weasel they'd caught, and that a whole family had been living up there. She said that sound—the mother weasel's final scream—was a warning to the father weasel and their children. *This house is dangerous . . . Don't stay here or they'll drown you . . . Leave and don't come back . . . Goodbye.* That's why we had to do it here, my grandma said. Now they'll never come back. And not just them. All their relatives, all the weasels in the area, they heard what happened. They know this house is the last place they want to be. Nothing to worry about. They won't be coming back. It's a good thing we got the mother, she said. When you get a baby, they just scream for help. Father weasels get violent and wear themselves out trying to chew through the cage before you can even get them in the water. The mother's the best, she said. Then she put her hands together again and kept praying. And that was the last of the weasels."

"What happened to the weasel's body?" Yoko asked, cheek in palm, eyes still closed. "I wonder," my wife said, cocking her head as she thought for a moment. "Maybe they really did throw it in the river." Then we stopped talking. A silence spread between me and the three drinkers. Saiki stared at the floor with a frown on his face. Yoko suddenly sat up and looked at my wife. Although the pot had been steaming up until a minute ago, a white film was starting to form around the edges.

One day, around the time the cherry blossoms finally bloomed in town, my wife's cell phone rang. "Oh, it's Yoko-san," she said as she hurried to pick up.

"Yeah. No, absolutely ... oh, it was delicious. Yeah? Hehe. Right? Really? You think so? I'm so happy to hear it."

If I didn't know any better, I would've thought the two of them were old friends.

"No. That's right. Only at the store. I'll bring more next time. Hehehe. Oh yeah? No, really, you don't have to ..."

They went on like that for some time. I could only imagine that they were talking about the sweets my wife had brought when we went to visit. "Well, you're always welcome here. Our house is nowhere near as big as yours, but we'd be happy to have you. Give my best to your husband," she said, then hung up.

"What was that? 'Thanks for the sweets'?"

"Uh-huh. That, and the weasels are gone."

I looked at my wife. She was smiling. My cell phone started vibrating, and Saiki's number appeared on the display. I still didn't know the results of the sperm test. My wife hadn't said a thing about having a baby since.

YUKIKO

YOKO HAD A BABY. IT CAME EARLY, AND SHE AND THE baby had to stay in the hospital for a while. My wife was there during the delivery. She was visiting Yoko, who wasn't due for some time, when things took a sudden turn. My wife drove her to the hospital. On the way, she comforted Yoko at every red light, holding her hand and speaking to her softly.

Saiki was out of town that day. He'd gone away for work. It was especially unfortunate because he'd set it up so he could be there with Yoko before she was due and during the birth. Apparently he was somewhere with no cell signal, and because he'd left without choosing a place to stay beforehand, there was no way to get in touch with him. Saiki hurried home when he heard the news, but by then it had already been a couple of days. My wife stayed at the hospital until Yoko's mother came, and had even taken a few days off work. "It's fine. Everyone's always taking time off to have kids or spend time with their children. I can take a couple of days, no problem," she said, full of excitement. But when Yoko's mother came from Yamagata and my wife's presence was no longer needed, she looked dejected. Despite the time that my wife had spent at the hospital, she still hadn't gotten a good look at the baby's face. Neither had I when I visited. The whole time I was there, she was in an incubator behind a pane of frosted glass.

★ ★ ★

Sometime after Yoko had left the hospital, we finally went to see their daughter. When we got in the car, we figured we'd arrive a little after noon and stay until evening. But as we made our way up the mountain, a light snow started to fall. It was the end of February, so it seemed likely that this would be the last snow of the winter.

When we pulled up to Saiki's place and got out of the car, I looked back at the tracks that the tires had left in the white snow collecting on the ground. Saiki came flying out of the house.

"I've been calling your cell, but you weren't picking up ..."

"Yeah, I was driving, I didn't notice."

"I was just wondering if it might be best to head back, with the snow and all ..."

The flakes of snow were as large as flower petals, but falling without a sound. It didn't seem bad enough to make us turn around and leave. We'd already come all the way out.

"I'm sure it'll stop in no time. Hey, you planted some new trees."

"Where's the baby?" my wife asked.

"She just went to sleep," Saiki said apologetically. "She was up and crying until a second ago."

"Hey, let's go inside. It's freezing."

"Oh ..."

When we stepped into the house, it was warm. The dining room was well insulated, with double-paned windows. A stifling heat was coming from the stove, but the cold still found its way in. There was a large teapot steaming on the stove. In the tatami room next to us, the baby was asleep. It was dark, so I only popped my head in for a quick look. Yoko saw my wife and broke into a smile.

"Thanks for coming. She finally went to sleep, just a second ago ... Sorry about that. She's probably going to be asleep for a while."

My wife let out a muffled squeal, then wrapped her arms around herself and said, "This is the first time I've seen her sleeping. At the hospital, the midwife wouldn't let me see her. She's so adorable."

I wasn't sure if what I'd seen earlier was the baby's face. Saiki took a seat, then stared out the window with a glum look. He'd put on some more weight.

"I don't know. We haven't had snow like this since we moved here. Last winter was warm. Hard to say how bad this'll get ..."

"That's true," Yoko said, nodding worriedly. The two of them seemed anxious, but my wife and I were unfazed.

"I'm sure it'll be okay. It'll let up before we drive back."

"Who knows," Saiki said, lifting his large mug and taking a sip, then cocking his head. Water bubbled in the full teapot. They had teacups set out for us. They were small, with Chinese-style pictures of boys balancing on balls. It looked like hojicha.

"How's work treating you?"

"Not too bad, but now I've got the baby to think about ..."

My wife turned to Saiki and said with a straight face, "Hey, your face looks like a dad's now."

"And it's not only his face," I said. "He's a real dad, from head to toe." Yoko laughed and my wife just shrugged.

The whole time we sat there chatting, my wife held on to the gift we'd brought. As I wondered when she was going to give it to them, Saiki said in a sharp voice: "It's a real snowstorm now. Guys, this is serious. You really shoulda ... Damn."

"Huh?"

I turned to look out the window and saw that the snow was no longer coming straight down. It was getting carried by the wind, beating sideways against the window. Still, I'd hardly call it a snowstorm.

"You've got to be kidding. This is nothing. They said on the news—"

"No, look at the snow. The flakes have gotten a little smaller, right? That's the kind of snow that sticks around—like it does in the north."

"But there's no reason they can't spend the night here with us. I'm sure the weather will be better tomorrow." At Yoko's words, my wife and I looked at each other in disbelief.

In the end, they were right. We couldn't make it home that night. The snow kept blowing, growing stronger as it covered the mountains in white. When we turned on the news, there was no mention of the weather we were seeing. It had to be a local storm, limited to the mountains around here. As we spoke, we kept our voices low so we wouldn't wake the baby in the next room. When my eye drifted in the baby's direction, I could see all kinds of things gathered around the crib: diapers, toys, soft-looking blankets.

"That's a lot of stuff. It's all for the baby?"

"Almost all of it came from our neighbors. A bunch of hand-me-downs. Most of it's got to be ten or twenty years old. They all bring whatever they've got. Random junk. Every day, somebody comes by with something new, and half of it we won't need for months ... But we don't have anywhere to put it, so we've just been leaving it out like this."

Outside the window, it was pure white. The baby was sound asleep.

"She's gaining weight every day, just a little," Yoko said happily to my wife. "We bought a scale for newborns. That way, we know her weight down to the gram."

"How's your milk?"

"Actually, it's been really good for a while now. The midwife had nothing but nice things to say. She said she was impressed. We don't need formula anymore."

Yoko's cheeks were looking fuller—not nearly as hollow as they'd been when she was in the hospital. But she did have rings under her eyes. She was wearing an open-front cardigan over a plaid shirt. Yoko's mother had apparently gone back to Yamagata a week earlier.

"Her mom disinfected the room for us. Thanks to her, we can rest easy."

"We've made a real mess, though . . ." Yoko added. As if those words had reminded her of the giant paper bag in her lap, my wife held our gift out for her.

"Oh yeah, I hate to add to the chaos, but . . ."

"What's this?"

"Nothing special. Just a little present."

"Oh wow." It was an imported wooden toy and some baby clothes. The two of them started talking excitedly about baby brands. When did they get so close? By this point, Yoko and my wife were probably better friends than Saiki and me. I took a sip of tea. The color was thin, but a bitterness spread around the base of my tongue.

The wind didn't stop and the snow only grew stronger. At some point, Saiki got up to make a phone call.

"It's Saiki. How are you doing over there? Yeah, who knew, right? Well, let me know if anything comes up. Oh, right . . . That's my friend's car. Not the best day for a visit, I know. Anyway, what do you think? Any chance they can make it home tonight?"

"Who was that?"

"Our neighbor. The old woman down the road. She's all on

her own, so I figured I'd better see how she's holding up, but you should have heard her. *Don't worry about me! Do you have any idea how many years I've been living out here?*"

"Sounds like a real character."

"Yeah. She's eighty-two," Saiki said, a pitiful look on his face. "Anyway, the verdict is in. She says there's no way you're leaving tonight."

Just as she predicted, by the time that the snowstorm had stopped, it was dark out, with well over five inches of snow on the road. I didn't want to try my luck on the mountain roads at night, with hardly any streetlights to guide the way, but my wife seemed ready to leave.

"I mean, with the baby and all ... We'd be putting you out. Isn't there someplace in the area where we could spend the night?" Her cheeks looked pale.

"It's fine, really," Yoko said firmly. "We wouldn't want you going anywhere else. You'll stay here. The baby can be pretty loud at night, but we'll set you up in the room at the other end of the house ..."

"Good idea. I'll go and clean up a little." Saiki heaved himself up, the baggy seat of his pants flapping as he went.

"But ..." my wife started to say, just as we heard what sounded like a siren in the distance. Yoko shot up and headed for the crib. From where I sat, I could see that the heels of Yoko's socks were threadbare. I felt kind of sorry for her. The crib was white, but by no means new. What I thought had been a siren was apparently the baby crying in the next room. Yoko picked her up, apologized, then shut the fusuma.

"I don't know, maybe we should have listened," I said as I scratched my head.

"Mmm, we took the mountain weather too lightly," my wife said.

Startled by the deep pitch of her voice, I realized how high it had been until then. She finished the tea in her cup and furrowed her brow. The makeup around her eyes had started to smudge. "I wonder if Yoko-san's feeding the baby," she whispered, her voice still low.

Outside the window, it was perfectly dark. There was something frightening about the bright snow beating against the window in the darkness. The storm was over, but the snow was still falling and a light wind was blowing. Meanwhile, the siren on the other side of the fusuma had stopped, and I could hear Yoko saying something in a low voice.

"It's good to know they're both doing well . . ."

"She's so small."

"Huh?"

The wrinkles on my wife's forehead deepened. "I know she said the baby's gaining weight, but she's so small. I wonder if the baby's really okay at home like this, if the milk she's getting is enough."

I thought back to the time we came for boar stew. Yoko had drunk a lot. But, thinking about the timing of the baby's birth, there was a chance that she was already pregnant. Maybe Yoko didn't know it yet, but that same thought ran through my head when I heard that the baby had come early. Apparently the weasels really hadn't been back since then. "Weasels probably carry a lot of germs, so it's good we took care of that before the baby was born. It's all thanks to you."

My wife gave a slight nod and looked outside. Her lips were dry and white. "I wonder if weasels hibernate during the winter."

"You don't know?"

"I've only seen a weasel that one time."

In the dark outside the window, I saw something bright green flash past. While I was still trying to figure out what I'd just seen,

I heard the front door slide open, then a voice. "Saiki-saaan."
Yoko and the baby were moving around on the other side of
the screen. I started to get up, thinking maybe I should see who
it was, but then I heard Saiki shout. "What's going on? Everything okay?" I heard footsteps rushing toward the door. "You're
covered in snow." It had to be the old woman from next door. I
could hear him thanking her, over and over. Yoko cracked open
the fusuma and looked out. I could see a little of the baby's head.
She didn't have much hair yet and her skin was red. After a little
while, I heard the front door open again. Through the window,
I saw the old woman in green pass by—this time with Saiki, who
was wearing a red down coat. Yoko shut the fusuma.

"She was feeding the baby just now."

"Oh yeah?"

"Yeah, I could see . . ." My wife stood up, grabbed the teapot
on the stove and filled her cup. Her face was hidden in steam.
"Hot water?" "Uh-huh." She pursed her lips and blew all the
steam away. The wind was whistling outside. "She was feeding
the baby."

"I'm back," Saiki said from the entryway. "Hello?"

Yoko didn't answer, so I got up and went to the door. Saiki
was doing his best to brush the snow off the hood and shoulders
of his bright-red coat. There was a large plastic container on top
of the shoe cabinet.

"Your car looks like a damn snowman out there."

"Look who's talking."

"Where's my wife?"

"In there."

"Feeding the baby? Changing diapers?"

Yoko came out with the baby in her arms. Maybe she'd heard
us talking. "Was that the neighbor?"

"Yeah, she brought some inarizushi."

"Oh wow." I looked at the baby in Yoko's arms. Her eyes were shut, but I could see her eyeballs. They looked like frogs' eyes, shifting beneath a translucent membrane. Yoko's skin looked like it was covered with a layer of pink cloth. Her shirt was misbuttoned, and her skin was showing through the gap. Saiki shook his soaked head.

"She made enough to share with us, but decided against coming over when it started snowing. Then she changed her mind when I told her we had company. She said she wanted us to have this."

Saiki took off his wet coat and hung it over the door.

"She made it herself?"

"Don't worry. She's a real fine cook."

Saiki was apparently no longer in the habit of calling her a hag. Holding the baby with one arm, Yoko left, then came back with a towel and handed it to Saiki. He gave his head a good scrub, then handed the tupperware to me. It was warm and heavy. When I tilted it, I could see a syrupy brown liquid inside, pooling at the bottom. Yoko shifted to get a better hold on the baby.

"She said the inarizushi would help you produce more milk."

"Oh yeah?"

"Yoko, where'd we put the oil heater? Is it in the back?"

"The oil heater?"

While the two of them started talking, I went back into the dining room. My wife was sitting up straight, still blowing on her tea.

"Inarizushi from the neighbor," I said as I put the container on the table.

"So it helps with your milk?" she asked and laughed. "Guess I'd better have some, too."

"You could hear?"

"The wind's blowing this way. But it's hot in here, isn't it?"
She rolled up the sleeves of her sweater. Dark-blue veins ran up
the skin of her arms. On her wrist was a thin watch I don't think
I'd ever noticed before. The seashell inlay gave the watch face a
slick, iridescent sheen.

Yoko carried the baby back into the tatami room, then called us
over to join her. I stumbled over what seemed to be a handmade
pull toy pieced together from bits of wood. The pull cord was
braided together from different colors of yarn. We sat down next
to the crib. My wife smiled at Yoko and asked, "Is it okay if I
hold her?" Yoko smiled back, said "Of course," then held out
the baby. The buttons on Yoko's shirt were still off, but my wife
didn't say anything.

My wife held out her hands and took the baby from Yoko,
then whispered the baby's name. "Yukiko-chan . . . Like the song,
right? 'Look at all the snow, my little Yukiko'?"

Yoko didn't know how to respond. I was confused, too. She'd
already told us the other day. The "Yuki" in her name meant
"joy," not "snow."

". . . Actually, it's 'Yuki' like happiness."

"What a pretty name. So cute."

"But maybe if she'd been born on a snowy day like today, we
would've gone with the other Yukiko."

The baby was silent in my wife's arms, her eyelids fluttering.
My wife looked at her, stuck her lips out, and mouthed something without making a sound. I had no idea when she'd put it
on, but her lipstick was a different color than before.

"She looks like you."

"She really does, doesn't she?" Yoko said as she smoothed the
sheet in the crib with her palm. "Honestly, I think she looks just
like me, more and more every day."

"Does Saiki help out with the baby?"

"Sure," Yoko nodded. "And he's almost always home for work. With breastfeeding and everything, I've got nothing left. I pretty much pass out during the day, and can't get any sleep at night. My rhythm is way off, but he's been weirdly healthy. He does everything from morning to evening, outside of feeding her. He never gets up during the night, though ..."

"Wait, so he changes her diapers?" When I was young, I would help with my sisters' kids or sing them lullabies, but I never went near their diapers. Even if we were related, it never felt right to wipe some baby's butt like that.

"He sure does. She's still drinking breast milk, so maybe it doesn't smell that bad ... But yeah, he does whatever has to be done."

"I'm shocked," I growled. The Saiki I knew wasn't the type who voluntarily took care of any child—even his own. I was pretty sure he didn't like kids. "Didn't know he had it in him."

"It isn't like that for women. Every baby is adorable to us ... But maybe it's different for men. They only see their own babies that way. Sorry, I shouldn't have ..." Yoko looked at me and held one hand over her mouth.

"No," I said. "Anyway, I think you're right. Maybe it doesn't affect us the same way. Maybe it should, but ..."

I glanced at my wife, but she was looking at the baby. It was like she couldn't even hear me. She was still moving her lips, but making no sound. *Yukiko ... Look at all the snow, my little Yukiko.* There was a futon spread out in a corner of the room. Yoko probably slept there at night.

"But I love kids. When I was about twenty, I was always happy to spend time playing with my sister's baby."

"Then why don't you take the baby?" my wife suddenly asked in a high voice, turning the baby in her arms toward me. "Is that okay, Yoko-san?"

"Sure, of course."

"You're sure you've had enough?"

"Mhm." Maybe my wife was trying not to disturb the baby, but she twisted her body awkwardly to hand the baby to me, her mouth weirdly contorted. The baby was actually heavy—a lot heavier than she looked. As soon as she was in my arms, her face scrunched up as if some unfamiliar smell had hit her nose. She opened her eyes and I smiled as I relaxed my arms. The baby stretched out her legs and kicked my arm. "Be sure to hold her neck." Yoko put her hand on my arm, correcting my form.

"She's a real cutie."

With her eyes half-open, the baby looked at me like she wasn't sure if she could trust me. I could see that her irises were the color of wild grapes.

"Can she see?"

Yoko tilted her head to the side.

"She can definitely see, but maybe not so clearly."

"It's usually from three months or so when babies really start to see. She can see, all right," my wife said firmly.

I peered into the baby's face. It was so small, but all the parts were exactly where they were supposed to be: two little nostrils, even the beginnings of her eyebrows ... This is how we all start.

"Well, what do you think of our baby girl?" Saiki asked as he tiptoed into the room, towel hanging around his neck.

"She's a beauty."

"Isn't she? I'm just glad she takes after her mom."

Saiki poked at his daughter's cheek. She moved her face a little.

"Hey, she looked at me," Saiki said in a voice I'd never heard him make. "You warm enough? All done sleeping for now?" The baby reacted to his voice, her face twitching as she turned her neck. Her hands started moving, too. I felt like she wanted her dad, so I held her out and Saiki took her easily. That's when I realized how tense I'd been. My forearms and palms were moist with sweat.

"That's right, dada's here."

"Dada!" I burst out laughing. "Of course," Saiki said with a straight face. "It's too hard for her to say anything else. I'm going to be 'dada' until she can actually talk." "Dada!" I couldn't hold back my laughter. My wife told me to keep it down, so I went back into the dining room. Saiki whispered something to Yoko, and she nodded a few times. My wife kept her eyes on the baby in Saiki's arms, moving her lips like before. I poured some hot water into my teacup and drank it. White steam rose from the cup in wild swirls. When I sat down at the table, the three of them and the baby looked like a bizarre Holy Family. Yoko looked down, let out a frustrated sigh, and rebuttoned her shirt.

We started dinner after seven. Saiki offered us beer and sake, but we said no. Saiki didn't drink, either. The baby had gone to sleep and was back in her crib.

"These look great!" my wife said. Once the inarizushi had been put on a platter, I could see that each one was as big as a fist. Their wet skins were packed full and smelled sweet. Yoko had made miso soup and set out pickles for us.

"The pickles came from our neighbor, too." Greens and light-brown radish. The radish looked withered, but the greens were fresh. We grabbed the heavy inarizushi with our chopsticks and put them on our own plates. When I took a bite, I could feel the skin give way between my teeth. Something rough spread over my tongue and mixed with my saliva. As it made its way down my throat, I thought I was going to choke. It wasn't rice inside. I couldn't spit it out, so I took another bite. It was too dry to be rice, but I was sure it was something I'd had before. My teeth and tongue told me that there were shredded bits of scallion and carrot mixed in. It tasted sweet and sour. When I finally got a mouthful down, I looked at Saiki and said, "This isn't rice, is it?" Saiki shook his head as he chewed, then said, "It's okara."

"Right, okara," I said, looking down at the giant inarizushi. I had only managed to eat maybe a fifth of it. My wife was smiling as she chewed. She swallowed and said, "It's seasoned just like sushi rice, isn't it?"

"Uh-huh. It's called azuma," Yoko said without missing a beat. She took another bite. "That's what our neighbor said. Well, azuma is seasoned okara wrapped in vinegared fish. This is like that—but inari."

"It's full of soy," Saiki said as he made short work of his piece. There was just a hint of vinegar amid the soy sauce and sugar. The scallions and carrots were almost raw.

"So that's why she said it was good for mother's milk. Soybeans ..." For her next bite, my wife took a mouthful. "It's really good."

"We aren't eating any carbs. Should I cook some rice? We have some in the freezer."

"Oh, this is filling enough. This'll be plenty."

I wanted rice, but I couldn't bring myself to ask. I didn't dislike okara, and I've always loved inarizushi. But expecting rice and getting bean pulp—sweet and sour like sushi rice, on top of that—left me feeling a little weird. I took a sip of the miso soup. It had gluten cake and green onion in it. It almost tasted like it came out of a package, but it was still better than the so-called sushi. When I finally finished my first piece, I moved on to the pickles. Both the greens and the radish were nice and vinegary. They tasted great. My wife had three pieces of sushi. Saiki and Yoko had more, too.

"That was so good. I wonder if I could ask your neighbor how to make it."

"I'll ask her next time."

"You've been treated to something special tonight. Real country cooking." Saiki grabbed a toothpick. I got one for myself and picked at a piece of scallion. My wife had another cup of tea. It seemed like the baby was already sound asleep.

When my wife finished her tea, she got up to stand by the crib. She was moving her mouth again as she looked down at the baby. Yoko did the dishes. Saiki spoke to me.

"Your futon's ready for later. It's a little cramped in there, but ... Come on, bring your stuff. I'll show you the room."

When I stepped into the room that Saiki had set up for us, white light flooded my eyes. Under a fluorescent lamp sat a row of rectangular fish tanks on steel shelves.

"I got started again," Saiki muttered, apparently embarrassed. "These are my tropical fish."

I counted five tanks—none of them very large—but the room was so small that they seemed to take up the whole space.

"At first, I thought I'd stick with one tank, but once I got going ... Anyway, we've got the room for them."

One aquarium was longer than the rest. There was a single fish in it, long and silver. "Hey, is that a bonytongue?" Saiki nodded. It definitely had the shape of one, but it was smaller and thinner than any bonytongue I'd seen before. It couldn't have been more than eight inches long. "It's pretty small—for a bonytongue."

"He's still growing. He's just a kid."

"Huh. Still, it has a real presence, doesn't it? You got it from the store?"

"Yeah, of course ... I'm going to have to get a bigger tank for him before long. If I take decent care of him, I'll have to get a six-foot tank eventually."

Of course, all the other tanks had fish and water in them, too. I guess this was Saiki's taste: no bright colors—no reds, no blues—only catfish and loaches resting at the bottom of their tanks among schools of little black fish. The bonytongue was the most eye-catching of them all, and it was almost completely still, its eyes wide open as it quietly moved its fins.

"Yoko-san didn't fight you on this? It must have cost you a lot."

"Actually, she was all for it. When she was pregnant, she'd come back here to nap ... Besides, it's not bad to have living things around to show the baby."

"But it'll be another three or four years before Yukiko-chan has any clue what they are, right?"

"If you showed her the bonytongue right now, she'd make a face like you wouldn't believe."

"Even though she can't really see yet?"

"Nah. She can see just fine. She can see what she wants to see."

The tanks were set up against the wall opposite the door, and the two futons were right in front of them, side by side. From the position of the pillows, it looked like we were going to be sleeping with our heads right by the fish. The gurgling of bubbles was constant.

"Is your bonytongue doing okay? I know it's winter and all, but it's barely moving. It doesn't move like a kid ..."

"This is how they are. He's fine. Sometimes I'll feed him live frogs, and you should see the way he moves then. In the wild, these guys jump out of the water to prey on insects. An adult can jump about three feet in the air. That's why I keep a cover over the tank."

"Has it ever jumped out?"

"Hell no. He'd die if he did."

I got in the bath first. Yoko had even put out a pair of pajamas for me to use. As soon as I was out of the bath, I felt like I was ready to go to sleep.

"You've got to be tired," Yoko said worriedly as she set out a jacket that looked like a chanchanko. It was clean, but smelled like old cotton. This was the first time in ages that I'd felt so tired.

"I don't think I can hold on any longer. I'm way too sleepy. I'd better turn in."

My wife didn't so much as glance in my direction. Her eyes

stayed fixed on the baby. After her bath, she came out in clothes that Yoko had lent her: a black shirt with a round neck—the sort of thing she never wore at home. She could hardly contain her excitement. It was almost funny, considering how worried she'd been earlier about imposing on them. Maybe women are happier to spend the night with friends than men are.

"Anyway, I'm going to bed. Good night."

When I got into bed, the sound of the water in the tanks by my head only made me sleepier. The snow was no longer beating against the window. A few times in my dreams, I heard a siren and saw my wife call the baby's name, feeding her at her breast. I was watching it from a distance. *Yukiko . . . Look at all the snow, my little Yukiko.*

I woke up hungry. I hadn't had a full dinner before going to bed. Just one piece of inarizushi filled with okara. It was a big piece, but it still wasn't enough. My stomach hurt. When I sat up, there was a faint light in the room. It must have been morning already. It looked like all the fish were asleep. My eyes weren't fully open yet, but I saw one small fish that looked just like a catfish on its side at the bottom of the tank. The pale red tips of the waterweeds were waving gently. When I brought my face up to the glass, it was warm. I could hear some sort of machine in motion—something like a motor. The fish were swaying in the water. The plants did the same. The air in the room was still. That was when I realized that my wife wasn't there.

The futon next to mine looked untouched, the comforter still neatly folded. The surface of the pillow was smooth, too. I reached for the curtains and pulled them back a little. It was completely dark out. Still night. Then what was all this light? I suddenly felt cold. Maybe it was only the bright white of the sheer curtains. Or maybe some faint light was reflecting off the water in the tanks, filling the room. I went back to the futon. I found my own body heat waiting for me, and once I'd pulled the comforter up to my neck, I could feel myself relaxing. If it was still night, then I couldn't have been in bed for long. My wife was probably absorbed in conversation with Yoko. It was too much trouble to check the time. When I closed my eyes to go back to sleep, I heard a splash. I tried to get up, but I couldn't move. I couldn't even open my eyes. I felt a weight on me, like something was pinning me down. It was so heavy over my stomach that it hurt. And it was cold. Moisture soaked through the comforter over my stomach and through my chanchanko, chilling my belly through my pajamas. My teeth chattered. My chest, face, and thighs were wet. The pressure on my belly was moving, sending water flying. I was in pain—like my body was being twisted by the weight and movement. Whatever it was, its narrow body was making rapid movements now. Then I realized: it was the bonytongue. It had jumped out of its tank and landed on me. Why wasn't the tank covered? And why did it feel so much bigger than it had looked? So much heavier? I tried desperately to open my eyes. I couldn't. I could feel the bonytongue twisting. It had to be in pain. If it died like this, Saiki was going to be upset. I didn't want this fish dying on top of me. I tried to raise my voice—to say something. I couldn't even get my tongue to move. I felt the sharp tail flapping against my belly. Light fluttered down like glittering scales behind my eyes, which were still sealed shut. I could hear a voice in the distance. A small voice, like a siren, a cry, some kind of prayer. In that moment, my body became light and I opened my eyes. I sat up. The bonytongue wasn't there. My futon was dry. The silver fish was in the tank above my head, motionless, only its eyes open. Its scales were shining. My wife was asleep beside me. Her closed eyelids were swollen, casting shadows over her cheeks. It had been a year, maybe longer, since

I'd last looked at my wife's sleeping face. Just beyond the glass, the small fish pulled together, their eyes set on me. The pale light of morning crept in from beyond the curtain.

I put my coat on and went outside. It wasn't morning yet, but the sky was already perfectly calm—like last night's snowstorm had never even happened. Before long, Saiki came out. When I saw him, I held up a hand.

"Did I wake you up?"

"No, I was up already—just doing a little work. I always wake up a lot earlier than I should. Just like an old man. Besides, with the baby and all . . ."

Saiki stretched happily. Where the sun had started to reach the snow, it sparkled like crystal, but the snow in the shade was frozen and dark. Saiki sighed, his breath shimmering as it caught the morning light. Under all the snow, my car looked like a giant stuffed animal. When I pushed my hand through the snow on the hood, it went all the way to my wrist. It felt oddly warm, then it started to sting. I pulled my hand back. I wondered if we'd be able to make it home today.

"Look how red your hand is," Saiki said as he scraped some of the snow on my car into a ball and tossed it at me. I ducked, then threw back a snowball of my own. I got him on the shoulder. Saiki brushed the bits of snow off and asked if the fish were too loud. "Some people can't sleep with the noise from the tanks."

"The sound was fine, but . . ." I said, then I told him about my dream. "I've never had an experience like that before. It was like I couldn't move, like the bonytongue wouldn't let me."

Saiki laughed, but it sounded more like a wheeze. "Damn. The curse of the bonytongue . . . I guess I shouldn't have said anything about it being able to leap out of the tank."

"I can't believe you had us sleep in there with that thing."

"Oh, come on. The tank was covered the whole time."

"You sure about that?"

"Of course I am. Besides, the fish isn't nearly as tough as you think. If something like that happened, the fish would be in a lot more pain than you. Think about it."

Think about the bonytongue. I had to laugh.

"But yeah, I can really see the appeal of tropical fish. Maybe I should get some of my own."

"Don't do it, man." Saiki's face turned sour. "It's a lot more work than you think," he said as he walked away.

"Why not?"

"I know they look pretty, but they're living things."

Saiki's black rubber boots left deep impressions in the snow. I followed behind him in my sneakers. The mountains in the distance were lit up by the sun, the light drifting like mist. It was getting lighter by the second. Saiki stretched again, his coat twisting along with the movement of his body. There was something striking about his red jacket in the light of the morning sun—it was so simple, so bright.

"That's some jacket."

"If you wear natural colors around here, you could get mistaken for a boar and end up getting shot."

Saiki launched a snowball into the air with everything he had. It flew a good distance, then fell perfectly intact. I heard the faint sound of snow hitting snow. I gathered some snow in my hands, then buried my face in it. Saiki said something. "What was that?" I asked as I pulled my face up. My nose tingled.

"It sounded like your wife was crying last night."

"What? Why?" I was pretty sure that she'd been in a good mood.

"I don't know. She was talking with Yoko and Yukiko in the other room ... But I'm pretty sure that's what I heard." Saiki put his hands on his waist and twisted side to side. I looked down at the snow in my hands, then I let it drop. It landed on my sneakers in an ungainly clump. I kicked my feet to shake it off.

"She's been really busy with work lately. It's definitely weighing on her. I know that. They have her working overtime every night ..."

"Hmm," Saiki looked at me. "Well, I know I'm not exactly Mr. Sensitive, and it isn't my place to say anything, but I was a little worried. If she's doing all right, then great. I'm glad to hear it. It's just, you know, the motions of the heart and all ..."

"What's that mean?"

"No idea." Saiki lifted his knees high as he trampled over the snow, shaking the slender trees as he went. Something black— maybe a butterfly or a moth—was falling among the flakes of snow, then suddenly flew up. The edges of its wings looked tattered, as if something had taken a bite out of it.

We circled around the snow-covered garden over and over. We saw our own footprints ahead of us. When we turned around, they were behind us, too. The more we walked, the more the snow turned to slush. It was becoming black. Once the color of the earth started to mix with the snow, it looked dirty. I rubbed my hands together. My palms were chapped and cracked. My lip had split open at some point, but I had no idea when. I could taste blood.

"This is nice."

Saiki's voice was so loud it startled me. He looked up at the snow gathered on the garden trees and said, "I know it wasn't the best timing for you, but it's nice to have some serious snow like this at least once a year." I heard a thud. Then the cawing of birds. A shrill cry: *peereereeree*. All of a sudden, the mountains and the trees were full of sound. It was still quiet in the house. Saiki looked down and tried to step perfectly into his own footprint.

When he got bored with that, he brushed the snow off things, starting with the bushes and the hose coiled up by the wall. I got into it and started doing the same. The branches and leaves were bare and withered. They looked gray. The white earth was getting dirtier. Cold moisture seeped in through the soles of my sneakers. I was about to tell Saiki that I was ready to go back inside when the old woman from next door came out and shouted good morning at the top of her lungs. Saiki shouted back, waving both hands in the air. I bowed. She was a really small old woman. Saiki stomped across the snow toward her. I followed him.

"Thanks for last night. That was delicious. Do you think you could tell Yoko how to make those?"

"Oh, that? That's just country cooking. Well, normally I'd use fish, if I had any ..." The woman broke into a grin and pointed at me. "Too bad about your car!" I scratched my head a little.

"There won't be any more snow today," she said firmly. "You'll make it home just fine. This is all going to melt by the afternoon."

"You think?"

"I know it," she said, then took a step toward me and almost whispered: "So—the woman who came with you ... Is that your wife?" I nodded. With a strange look in her eyes, the woman said, "She's got a baby on the way ..." When I widened my eyes and stared back at her, a grin spread across her face as she said, "You best take care. It's still early on." Early on? Out of the corner of my eye, I saw Saiki at a distance, playing with a ball of snow. The woman looked up at me as she spoke.

"Don't let the baby get cold. Nothing's worse than the cold. Take Yoko's belly wrap when you go home. I knitted it myself." The woman grabbed my wrist with her spotted hands. I could feel her short, bony fingers on my skin. They were warm. I tried to pull away, but her soft fingers were clenched tightly around my wrist and wouldn't let go. Then, in a low voice, she said, "It's up to both of you to look after the baby. You'll have to come back and say hello again, the three of you. Children are such a treasure—a gift to us all. So adorable, just like little Yukiko."

I stood there, unable to say anything.

"Take good care," the woman said, then went inside.

Saiki had made a snowman small enough to fit in the palm of his hand. "Hey, check it out," he said. His cheeks and fingers looked as red and swollen as the baby I'd held in my arms the night before. Saiki had drawn a face on the snowman with the tip of his finger. "Cute, right?" I nodded, but I wasn't sure what I was nodding at. "I'll have to show Yukiko. Better keep it in the freezer for now." There was no trace of night now. In the white light of day, the snow began to melt. I felt frozen from head to toe. On the road in front of the house, there were already tire tracks and a trail of footprints. They were headed up the mountain. I heard the faint sound of a siren.